LISTEN TO THE THORN BIRDS

*a melody in piercing agony,
a journey through pain and resilience*

Pratibha Panghal

NewDelhi • London

BLUEROSE PUBLISHERS
India | U.K.

Copyright © Pratibha Panghal 2024

All rights reserved by author. No part of this publication may be reproduced, stored in a retrieval system or transmitted in any form or by any means, electronic, mechanical, photocopying, recording or otherwise, without the prior permission of the author. Although every precaution has been taken to verify the accuracy of the information contained herein, the publisher assumes no responsibility for any errors or omissions. No liability is assumed for damages that may result from the use of information contained within.

BlueRose Publishers takes no responsibility for any damages, losses, or liabilities that may arise from the use or misuse of the information, products, or services provided in this publication.

For permissions requests or inquiries regarding this publication, please contact:

BLUEROSE PUBLISHERS
www.BlueRoseONE.com
info@bluerosepublishers.com
+91 8882 898 898
+4407342408967

ISBN: 978-93-6261-569-5

Cover design: Rishav Rai
Illustrations: Ankita Ghosh
Poet's Photo: Nikhilesh Badhwar
Typesetting: Rohit

First Edition: October 2024

Dedicated to my beloved parents in heaven

ਕੁੰਵਰ ਵਿਜੇ ਪ੍ਰਤਾਪ ਸਿੰਘ
Kunwar Vijay Pratap Singh
MLA, Amritsar North
Advocate, Punjab & Haryana High Court
MA, LL.B, MBA, Ph.D (GNDU Amritsar)
Former IPS (Punjab Cadre, 1998 Batch)

Member
Punjab Vidhan Sabha

Dated... 20.04.2024

FOREWORD

"Listen to the Thorn Birds" a poetry book by Mrs. Pratibha Panghal is a strong reminder of the strength that lies within the ordinary amidst a world yearning for remarkable things. A former school teacher, who writes in English, Hindi and Punjabi among other languages, her poems distil the humanity into rare expertise by encapsulating experiences.

Mrs. Panghal touches on love, loneliness and deceit which affect each one of us while displaying latent intricacies associated with human nature. She also successfully broaches social issues such as environmental pollution, family violence and gender partiality through verse making it meaningful and unassuming.

What differentiates this masterwork from others is that she can derive awe-inspiring moments from ordinary life events. Her poems are more than just lamentations or calls to motivate action but rather about happiness as well as resilience. Through these words, she gives readers a glimpse into otherwise mundane settings or objects; such as a small girl walking on a tight rope or even lone red bench where people sit to relax their mind after hard tasks of the day but the underlying meaning of the same is much deeper.

The raw emotional honesty that permeates each line and the poetic mastery will strike you as you delve into the pages of "Listen to the Thorn Birds". Mrs. Panghal's voice is a testimony to how enduringly effective words can be in capturing human experiences and helping us refocus on new ways of seeing.

We wish that this book will prove to be a testament to the transformative potential of the common masses, who can add their own unique cadence to the grand symphony of human expression. For in doing so, we too can become an extraordinary voice amidst the ordinary.

Kunwar

Kunwar Vijay Pratap Singh
MLA, Amritsar North
MA, LLB, MBA, Ph.D (GNDU Amritsar)
Advocate- Punjab & Haryana High Court
Former IPS (Punjab Cader, 1998 Batch)

Kunwar Vijay Pratap Singh

(M.l.A. Amritsar North)

Should our greatness stop us from experiencing and appreciating ordinariness?

Contents

When You Hug My Prayers 1

Listen To The Thorn Birds 2

The Women Within 5

The Past 6

Love 7

Dog And The White Snake 8

Doors And Windows 11

Not A People Whisperer 12

Children Of Dust 15

The Magician And The Children 17

Advice Whisperers 18

The Pied Piper 19

The Lone Red Bench 21

A Heart With Holes 22

Misprinted Hash Tag 24

Trying To Write Poems 25

No More Private Gardens 26

Mountains 27

Partiality 28

Depression 28

Bougainvillea 31

Paradoxes 32

Salvaging Rainbows 35

Don't Play With Fire	36
No Dice	37
The Elephant On My Ceiling	38
Time	41
Albatross	42
Weary Winters	45
Flamboyant Fall	46
Rains!	49
Inheritance	51
Summer Repose	53
Spring Buoyancy	55
That Room	56
Palm Reading	58
Spring Without You	60
Deafening Silence	61
She Walks The Tight Rope	63
They Only Wait	65
On Ageing	66
Flashback	69
Do You Remember?	70
Punctuation	71
Legacy Of Shattered Dreams	73
Inseparable	75
Things Left Behind	77
Elephant Woes	81
Water	83

Vaccine For Violence 84

Will You Be Here? 86

Quo Vadis World?..88

Go Into The Dark..90

Unsaid Words..91

An Ordinary Woman 92

The Trees Die 95

Words..98

Life Defined 99

When You Hug My Prayers

Each broken atom

Each drowned breath

Vibrates

In sync

With the cosmic rhythm

When You hug

All my humble prayers

Impossible dreams

Releasing these gently

Into the wind

Unto the clouds

Atop the mountains

Astride the waves

And I rise

On the wings of

Your glory

Becoming a beautiful

Miracle Of Your Love

And Benevolence

Listen To The Thorn Birds

Singing our sorrows

And joys

Rhythmizing desires and demons

Muddled together

We glide on notes

High and low

Orchestrated by life

Self created illusions

Of greatness

Of joy and abundance

These songs serenade all we are

And all we aren't

Ignoring, justifying

The cost of Creation

Mesmerized by

Fatal ambitions

Perching, pressing

Against thorny branches

We sing songs of life

With full throated mighty music

The sharper the piercing

Louder the song

Drenched in blood

Hypnotized by our

Own immortal chords

Magnificent mortal beings

Fading away

Yearning for immortality

Suffering suicidal symphonies

We hug Multipronged thorns

Floating on melodic designs

Embracing pain

To be heard and acknowledged

Listen to us

We are the Thorn Birds!

The Women Within

Coercion won't force
Them down
Deception can't
Stifle them
Emptiness fails to
Harden their lush desires
Into frigid flakes of indifference
I try to keep them imprisoned
For your sake
But they spill out of my palm
Defying destiny
The women in me

They want it all
Love, respect, hope
They chase it all
The stigma of age
And ugliness
Your silence
And contempt
Can not snub them
They want it all
The women in me

The Past

Always the black sheep

Notoriously hated

Belittled

Brushed under the carpet

With camouflaged threats

The villainous past!

But it's history too

A treasure chest

Of memories

A springboard

To evolution

A picturesque canvas

Of moods and moments

To be embraced

And accepted

Explored and valued

The past is priceless

Love

Love a pilgrimage

To places unknown

Within hearts and souls

Through intricate emotional labyrinths

Of pain and pleasure

Dreams and despair

Some get lost

Some surface

The journey never ends

Dog And The White Snake

It sat curled up

In scaly layers

On the floor

Just where my bed ended

Looking at me

In rapt concentration

The massive white snake

Alone in my room

I didn't know

What to do

The screams stifled

In fear

Body petrified into stillness

Suddenly my dog

Came rushing in

And stood between me

And the white entity

He, my dog
Has yet not learnt
To respect the
'Do not Disturb' signs
I ran out
But stood in the courtyard
Looking back at the scene
In my room

The beast and the being
Glaring at each other
Doing nothing!
The snake listless
At the unwanted
Change of prey
And my dog
Undecided about
Which layer to bite first

Drenched in sweat
I woke up
The dog lying at my feet
Snoring slightly
The nightmare ended

But isn't over

Every night

I see the scaly layers

And hug my dog even closer

While the house follows

Religiously

The ritual of isolation

Doors And Windows

Tall doors and wide windows

Make concrete chambers

Bearable

I can still breathe in

Rain sprays and sun streaks

Imprisoned emotions eagerly

Grasping scents of breezy earth

Can still relive fluent freedom

My stretched imagination

Can give wider dimensions

To my narrow choices

Tall doors and wide windows

Make concrete chambers bearable

Not A People Whisperer

I talk to trees

And birds

I understand what

Dogs say

And why cats look at us

In wonder

I can merge with

The wind

And the rain

And hug the sky

But am ostracized

By people

I cannot appear when they beckon

And vanish when

They alienate

I cannot

Say all the clever things

They want to hear

Nor can seal my lips

On demand

I cannot read their thoughts

Or escape their feelings

I wish I could

But am not

A people whisperer

Children Of Dust

We are the children of dust

We choose freedom

Over rat traps

Simple Joys over big

Dreams of gold

We own our time

We don't pawn it

To lick

Borrowed drops of dew

We are the children of dust

The Magician And The Children

One jerk of the black clad arm

And

Out flew White fluttering wings

Doves everywhere!

After the applause

A few children

Approached the magician

Holding out one dove

With a broken wing

'Magical new wings please

Give her the freedom to fly again'

The magician

Looked at the children

And the injured bird

He smiled

Then frowned

And turned away

Advice Whisperers

Move on!
Don't wait for the
Final blow
Don't let them steal
Your sunshine

Wait!
Don't be hasty
Be practical
Adjust and compromise
Avoid a lonely life

The advice whisperers
Grow more guttural
With each twilight
Their presence
Non avoidable

Judgemental pecking
Enjoying morsels of my
Weakening mind
The dark lights
Invading all dungeons
I collect my bits and pieces
Wriggling away painfully
Liberation doesn't
Come cheap

The Pied Piper

With Quaint wrinkled mind

But charming skills

The pied piper

Entices naive hearts

And they compete

Mercilessly

To be his chosen ones

Trampling upon bodies and beings

To follow him

Into the cavernous servitude

Wasting them away

Morsel by morsel

To feed his freedom

The Lone Red Bench

The lone red bench

Absorbing

Sunset hues

Splash by splash

Heaving a peaceful sigh

After callous traffic

Merciless pollution

And gnawing drumming

Of a hot summer day

Ready to slip into

A comatose night

With an old beggar

An orphaned child

Or a random stray dog

Hugging its comfort

Till the soothing sunset

Dons its blazing avatar

Again

Crushing starlit dreams

Into slithers of sharp reality

A Heart With Holes

"Look there is a heart

In your cup of coffee!"

He smiled

And my soul

Got lulled again

By the opium of hope

Another look at the cup

Raised goosebumps

Of fear again

The white heart floating

In the browns of coffee

Had holes in it!

Not one, but four!

I shushed my despair

And drank in

The white heart

With four holes

Reaching home
His smirks peeled away
The mask of cordiality
And the hiss was back on

'Am sleeping in the
Other room'

The heart with holes started
Churning inside me
Threatening all
Sucking all
Into its widening holes

I rushed into the washroom
Trying to throw it out

But it had embedded itself
Deep into the crevasses
Of my own wrinkled heart

And now
I have two hearts
With holes

Misprinted Hash Tag

Another horizon

Another time

Life speeds up

I stagnate

Isolated destiny

A tight cocoon

Searching the dry desolation

For lush portals

All lights up

Bathing me in

Dark layers of oblivion

The stillness

Tainting all that was pure

All that was sacred

Shadows glare at me

With mockery and disdain

Love – still

A misprinted hash tag

Trying To Write Poems

2 a.m.

Curled in with chilly darkness

And gnawing loneliness

Sleep a distant dream

I try to write poetry

Words and phrases

Zoom in and fade away

My mind a black hole

Sucking all

Releasing nothing

I feel a poem

But cannot touch her

Closer curls the darkness

And I leave the poem alone

No More Private Gardens

You scraped away my name

From the perch

You had created for me

Within your heart

And yes

I remember

'You will live

In my stomach forever'

You had told me then

Now, dwells in your stomach

A poison tree

With my name tag

And am still

Standing still where time had

Offered me a dream

Of gardens

Private villages

With our names

Floating on the bars of

A white bench

Mountains

Sometimes the mountains

Just eat you up

All that is fine is foggy

All that is kind is harsh

You lose trust in goodness

In people who mean well

The isolation hypnotizes

To see only the dark

The rocks harden the heart

The wind takes you

Far-far away from reality

Movement becomes a habit

And you don't stay

You only walk away

Breaking others

Into fragments

Never to be whole again

Sometimes

The mountains eat you up

Partiality

Justice

No thoroughfare

 In an air tight patriarchy

Male bastion

Keeps its blood sucking

Zombies safe

No fair deals

For the fair sex

She can claim sale tags

Not rights

Seeking dignity

Incurs fatal penalties

Depression

Sometimes

The angels you walk with

Are stalked by sadness

And all hues

Get sucked into the

Black hole of depression

Each call for help

Gets labelled as drama

All drift away

Leaving you alone

With your pain and vacuum

Bougainvillea

A lazy winter afternoon

The sun smiling down

At the delightful pinks

And sensuous reds

Of the bougainvillea

Still in its infancy

Faint fragrances

Softening the wings

Of a sleepy wind

The terrace

But an instrument

Reciting the pitter patter

Of my dog's excited paws

Paradoxes

Eager to share

The music and joy

Flowing from reverberating

Hands and feet

Fragrantly luminous dresses

And bright faces

At the pre wedding celebrations

Of my friend's son

I sent the pictures

And videos

To my cousin

And as a footnote

One of mine too!

'Why sadness in your eyes?'

My phone screen

Flashes her response

Jolting me out of

The pretence

That's been my only

Introduction to happiness

For a long time now

Am fatigued', I tell her
Knowing she would
Sense it is my soul
Am referring to
Hoping she might
Venture to hug my piranhas
And release my soul
Offering much needed catharsis
To be happy once again

Salvaging Rainbows

You rushed headlong

Into my heart

And life

With artistic strokes

And poetic endearments

Ecstatic that my dusty rainbow

Would now reflect colours again

I welcomed you with pure acceptance

Least knowing

That you were scrounging

For rainbows of your own

My dusty rainbow

Was soon coloured red

Bleeding beneath your smart claws

Trying to salvage

What was left

I lost my all

Don't Play With Fire

Everyday she

Teased the fire

Playing with its passion

Ruffling its infernal flames

Trying to calm its fury

She wanted a playmate

Who didn't roar or burn

But offered

Fragrant whiffs

Of warmth

The fire fretted and fumed

Tired of the everyday nagging

And with one stroke

Consumed all the oxygen

She breathed

No Dice

Your love for me
You have canned and dumped
Somewhere untraceable
Long ago

Many a torturous
Labyrinths I waded through
But could retrieve it not

The last dice
Rolled out by life
Annihilating
The nervous wait
For hope to be
The season of my heart
Time
Just a conundrum

I accept
The live murder
Of all that is pulsating within
And wait for the pall bearers

The Elephant On My Ceiling

Times like this

I talk to the baby elephant

On my ceiling

Silence screaming loud

My dog asleep

At my feet

My old father

Already turning into dust

Staring at his ceiling

Waiting to go

And love, always my desire

Could never be my destiny

Alone

Feverish

I miss my mother

And her warm hugs

Assuring smiles

Sitting straight

I stare

At the dim shape

Of a squatting baby elephant

On my ceiling

Where repairs have

Left grey marks

Creating a silhouette

Of a baby elephant

With a long trunk

The concrete discourages cuddles

So I talk to him instead

Pouring out the burdens within

I tell him all my tales

Unveiling the fissures

Of time

Digging deep into my heart

Singing to him

Songs prohibited

Emotions blocked

He sits there

Listening silently

I feel him nodding

His trunk bobbing up and down

I imagine pain on

His pure face

But all the time

He listens

I can talk to him

Endlessly

I lapse into silence

Am interrupted

My dog stirs

He is lonely too

I pat him back to dreams

And relapse

Back into my nightmares

Time

When time grinds it's teeth

To chew every joy

Out of your being

Each atom around becomes carnivorous

All mimic it

When it's cruel

All are unfaithful

When time betrays you

Albatross

Echoes

Screams and pleadings

Still haunt me

Your vacant eyes

Pierce me when I close mine

Cancer claimed all

You were

And all you could be

While doctors praised

Your courage

And friends embraced

Your kindness

I saw your erosion

Your pain and confusion

No fear of death

But the tumultuousness

Of leaving me behind

Among wolves and devils

I couldn't not save you

From cancer

Or worries

I could not make your

Passing away peaceful

And the echoes haunt me

The Ancient Mariner's curse of

Life-in-death falls heavily

On my fragile soul

I am the Albatross

Around my own neck

Weary Winters

Numbing nights devour
Faint remains of the day
Dark hearts
Unlit by light
Every thud, a scream

Chilly Fear
Splashing gory monsters
On all walls
Home turning into
Petrifying prison
Opening up dungeons of depressing depths

Loneliness lurks in every corner
Fog blurs vision and vigour
Longings for sunshine
Grow desperate by the hour
But
Grey boundaries don't allow
Light freedom
Winter smells like a graveyard
Death dictates life

Flamboyant Fall

Cruising towards

A tiny island

On the wide lake

Fall spurs into being

Spreading eclectic tangerine hues

The tall Chinar

Spraying amber golds

On the island floor

Colours rustle beneath our feet

Soft Sounds merging with faint scents

And strong hues

Autumn and paradox

Go together

Lazy birds perch on barren branches

Waiting for change to stir up all

And confusion rules hearts

Fall is a non sure time

Leaves undecided between

Orange pellets and golden ones

Nature keen on Spring

Yet rushing towards winters

Time writ large with

Billboards

'To hope or not to hope'

Rains!

Heartbeats break out
Into joyful dance
Raindrops pouring
Pulsating passion
Onto all life
Lovers merge
Their juvenile tunes into
Cosmic music
Wooing each other voguishly

Earth opens up
Receiving and reviving
Nature's magic
Rain washes away tears
Faint forlorn hearts flutter
To hop and hope again
Shining raincoats
Re define blurring wet streets
Community dogs
Hide under cars
And children
Play puddle games

Delicious savories

Fill homes and hearts

With pleasant scents

Paper boats carry

Dreams to destination

Magnetic Monsoon hugs all

Inheritance

We inherit pain

From someone

And somewhere

We cannot disown it

Nor can gift it

It clings till the end

And beyond

Summer Repose

Howdy to handsomely

Glorious times

Goodbye to gnawing chills

Summer offers a full plate of

Sunshine and shimmer

Sweet fruits and tangy juices

Tongue tingling iced Lollies

Invigorates parched minds and bodies

Hot moments just short interstices

Before recurring breaths of fresh sparkles

Ever broadening hours

Allow comforting slumber

And nostalgic brooding

Summer the liberator

With sparkling wand

Touches all

Bathing all

In warm embrace

Spring Buoyancy

Open bright days
Blowing away
Winter bleakness
Spring arrives
Garbed in stylish visuals

Multi hued blooms
Burst forth with wide smiles
Mornings offer
Free tickets to birds'
Musical concert
And days spread their horizons
To accommodate more joy

Sky repaints itself
Shining brighter, bluer
Trees shake off the chilly slumber
Hugging revived life
Dying hopes nudged to life again
As Nature re oxygenates all

That Room

The sinking floor

Of red bricks

A wide open door

With no curtains

Rotting beams overhead

Lizards' playground

Two windows

Painted lemon

By me and a friend

Long lost since

A narrow cupboard

With

My juvenile book collection

The big peepal tree

Outside the window

Rain trapped

In its soft leaves

Gusty walls wearing

Lively posters

A record player

And pictures

For sound and smiles

Freedom from sorrow

Ties of love

Co-existing in simplicity

That Room

Was blessed!

Palm Reading

He looks at my palm
The aged astrologer
Leaning across the table
Frowning away ruefully
My breathless expectations

Doodles on a yellow
Piece of paper and
Leans back In composure
My dying hopes
Flutter and
Dare to breathe again!
"Your Saturn is bad
So is your Sun and Venus"
A bounty of the 'bad' words
Slithor out of his mouth
I wait
For a change
In the tone and mood
Of his predictions

He leaves my palm

And spreads his-

It's payment time!

Stupefied, I struggle

To find my voice

'Please tell me about

The good too pandit ji'

After the hint of a sad smile

He wears the frown again

'All the 'good' in your destiny

Has vapourised

Long ago!'

The frown mocks at me again

I give up

Fill his palm

And go back to the void

Hugging my empty one

Spring Without You

Spring without you
Blossoms
Half heartedly
Reluctant to dance around
Just creeps bit by bit
Afraid to enter my heart
Steering away from the
Cactuses that grow there now
Sapping all fertility
Draining all vibrancy
Dark premonitions
Block all the sunshine
And the delicate canvass
Cringes in retreat
Yet hope
The stubborn, stunning hope
Grows wings
Flying above the barrenness
Beyond thorns and murk
Yearning to create magic
To open all closed doors
And let Spring dance
Its way back into my heart

Deafening Silence

Your silence

Screams loud

So voluble

So portent

Drowning all my words

Clouding all meaning

Erasing

Stroke by stroke

The unsaid words

The corpses of my protests

Fill my being with

Malicious stench

Each breath an ugly whisper

Each pulse beat –

Sheer helplessness

It's a hard battle

Silent noises

Overpower all!

She Walks The Tight Rope

Tiny feet

Grasping the thin rope strongly

Hands still in infancy

Holding a fully grown

Wooden pole

The only support

Against falling

To death

The girl child

Balancing all

To survive

Her anxious mother

On solid ground moving

In sync with her

Jerky walk on the tight rope

And father trying to

Attract more alms

Through rancorous singing

Remind me of another time

Another scene

Tiny feet decorated with henna

Washed and touched for blessings

On an auspicious day

Multi hued glass bangles

Wrapped around the wrist

And plates full of

Tasty offerings

Celebrating the girl child!

Am jolted out of my reverie

By my rikshawalla

Watching

The tight rope walk with me

He asks, 'Pair dho ke poojna

Phir kyuon rolna?'

(Why maltreat the same girl

Whose feet you wash, worshipping her?)

They Only Wait

Those who hope

Those who trust

Those who pray

Those who are incapable of evil

Keep on waiting

They don't want revenge

They don't want control

They wait for love

They wait for peace

Everywhere

For everyone

On Ageing

No, I am not in a hurry
To age
Don't push me
Don't hasten me
Let me take my time
Let me be
Alive right now

My horizon
Might conjure up
A few rainbows still
And the sun might carve out
A few more dawns

I don't like the sunset
Don't goad me
To grab one

I can hear hope
Singing to me
And love bathes my heart in

A warm glow, still

The wrinkles

The sagging body

The aches and pains

The hissing medical reports

Are not my identity

Not me

My heart is

My dreams are

Karma can contour

My fate still

Life might throw

More adventures my way

The path is not all erased yet

Let me walk

If not run

Let me put my mark

On a few more milestones

Don't push me off the cliff

Please don't tell that

I am a nobody now

Please don't hammer me

With 'your life is over' refrain

Please, please!

Let me live a little more

Let me hope a little more

Don't age me

Before ageing

Flashback

That morning

Your hands on my wrist

Playing with my

Red glass bangles

Orchestrated thousands

Of love poems

Millions of love songs

I still feel the reverberations

Each time I wear red bangles

Each time I look at your hands

I feel it all

Though we are strangers now

An ordinary middle class man
Who had ridden a bicycle
Till his legs gave up
Whose only claim
To travel had been
A few visits to relatives
And who could
Never publish a book
Opened all floodgates
Tearing me up
His silent desires
Finding a voluble
Release in my incoherent
Prayers for mercy
The box has remained
Unopened since then

Inseparable

I have woven

My fragile soul

Into your vastness

Spark by spark

Shadow by shadow

Separation now

Excoriates all that I am

Things Left Behind

A 'Thank you' note to me

In your diary

My Maa

Red orange pink bangles

Blessings

From temples

You were so fond off

And the multi coloured mugs and plates

You collected browsing through

The mall in wheel chair

A fortnight before you turned to dust

Your favourite Yardley powder

And nail paints

You always wore cheerfully

Things you left behind

Things I touch, smell and cry

Things I won't part with till

I too turn to dust

You send messages

From heaven now

Floating on wind and water

Spreading your hues and fragrance

In blooms on our terrace

Birds on the Ashoka tree

And

Paper boats in monsoon puddles

I embrace all

I embrace all the things

You left behind

All the messages you send

'I will never be far from you'

Your promise on death bed

Echoes all around me

Dimensions of your

Physical grace

Slipped from my embrace

But this

Love alive

Resounding through all

Layers of atmospheres

Peripheral boundaries

Between angels and the mortals

There's nothing like this anywhere

A love like this is immortal

Elephant Woes

He plods the asphalt

On his delicate foot pads

With broken toe nails

In heat and cold

Ducking electric wires and hanging billboards

His skin discolored with

Frequent maltreatment

Opaque eyes

Brimming with pain

And begging for mercy

Horrific training methods

Written all over his soul

Paraded in narrow streets

And coarse roads

Alienated from his family and friends

He misses the trees and rivers

The peace and comfort

Of his friendly habitat

Navigating a hostile territory

Cankerous sounds

And crude beings

He suffers unbearable torture

Psychological abuse and inhuman neglect

The beastly imposters parading him

In the name of gods

Glare at me when I refuse

To offer them money

And tell them to free

The innocent creature

I complain to the authorities

But they pay no heed

The elephant continues to be paraded

Amidst blind minds

Water

Please place water bowls
And troughs for them!
'No need
They find plenty in drains
And puddles'
But
Birds begin to vanish
With parched throats
And burnt wings
Puppies, aged dogs
Die wreathing in pain
The drain water
Injecting poison into the weaklings

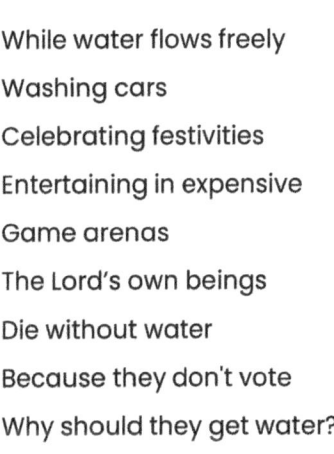

While water flows freely
Washing cars
Celebrating festivities
Entertaining in expensive
Game arenas
The Lord's own beings
Die without water
Because they don't vote
Why should they get water?

Vaccine For Violence

A dog enters a building

Hungry, thirsty, injured

His eyes a heart rending mirror of

Helplessness and fear

'Chase him away'

Shouts the owner

And the gatekeeper hits

The puny being with an iron rod

He tries to run away but death claims him

Mother bird bringing food for her hatchlings

Finds neither her babies nor the nest

With pitiful cries it flutters around

In vain

The home owners have cleared all

'It was spoiling our decorative garden'

Their excuse when the youngest child asks

About the birds he loved so much

'Principal of a reputed school shot by a student'

'Old parents locked in house by greedy son demanding property'

'A two year old molested'

Thus scream news headlines

Life unleashes Karma and Nemesis

Rampant everywhere

Avoidable violence

Unnecessary cruelty

Failure of education

Parents' neglect

To instill in impressionable minds

Kindness and empathy

The only antidote to

Wild growth of harshness

The only vaccine for

The pandemic of violence

Will You Be Here?

Post retirement

Post losing my father

Earth below my feet

Is all slippery sand

All uncertain terrain

The overcast sky

A hostile canopy

Sans sunshine

Sans stars

All my rainbows

Abducted by tenacious times

Sometimes soon

It will be time to

Walk those last steps

Towards nothingness

Will you be here

To hold my setting sun

In your embrace

And lower it gently

Into the soft earth

Its hues your colours

Its fire your warmth

And its oblivion

Your reincarnation

Quo Vadis World?

Behold the ripped mask

And the ugly virus within

Listen to the ruckus of

Hollow words beneath the lies

Feel the tentacles of

Octupian minds strangle

Your soul

See how the mighty fall

And thunder

The erosion is slow

You see yourself

Being wasted

Heartbeat by heartbeat

You hear the crunch

Of those beastly fangs

Sinking deep into your being

Savoring the bloody chunk

That was once your dignity

The loud guffaws of triumph

Tear through

All you held close

All you thrived on

The gloating guile

Sucks away all

There is no hatred within

Only pain and confusion

Go Into The Dark

You have to go
Into the dark
Alone
There is no hand to hold
And no light to lead

You have to go into the dark
Alone
There is no other way
And no excuses left

You have to go into the dark
The fireflies are all dead
You are alone
You have to go into the dark

Unsaid Words

Voluminous words gush out

Of mouths and mobiles

Expressing so much

Telling nothing

Clouding all meaning

It's the unsaid word

Where the truth lurks

Hiding meekly

An Ordinary Woman

No talent

No claim to greatness

Dumb face

And boring personality

Simple dreams

Of happily ever after

Ordinary joys and sorrows

She didn't want the sky

And the stars

But to walk the earth safely

And with dignity

Wasn't searching for

A soul mate

Just someone kind and caring

To grow old with.

To feed the dogs and doves together

Laugh at silly jokes

And tuneless singing

Of the self, together

Was her idea of love

The courage to love

After heartbreaks

Had given her

Extraordinary punishments

When death claimed her

She just passed away ordinarily

The Trees Die

A tree executed

And another

It goes on...

The altar of progress

Claims great sacrifices

Ropes tied around

To stifle life

Out of earth's lungs

Even before they fall

Lush green leaves

Tremble in fear

Clinging desperately

To the creaking branches

Affording no haven

In last hopes for dignity

The trunks try to stand erect

Under the strokes

Of the merciless axe

With a last glance heavenward
Praying for mercy, finding none
They fall to the cold ground
Dead logs
Once, a pulsating tree!

Mother earth lets them go
Helpless, powerless

And the trees go
One by one
Without a goodbye

No leaves will dance
On the rhythmic winds
No birds would grow families
And squirrels will abandon
Playful antics
The massacre complete
A graveyard born

Mindless genocide
Leaves a verdant, vibrant spot
Bleak and barren
Nature mourns in silence

The tragedy gets repeated

At another place, everywhere

Regiments of Concert

Jungles devour

Earth's vitals

Igniting premature extinction

Of God's domain

And all remain silent

Doing nothing

Words

Words express, impress
Even depress
Question, answer
And confuse

Words, versatile words
Inform, reform
Transform
Co-relate, communicate
Separate

Words work overtime
Effortless artisans
Vibrate, initiate
Invigorate

Words, magical words!
Powerful tools
Overpowering masters

Yet incomplete
Insufficient, ineffective
Without action.

Life Defined

Arid winds, parched destiny

Timbered hearts, up in smoke

Rare rains, tiny puddles

Cool silhouettes

And half filled scoops of joy

Messages

To write a good poem, it is very important to be a good person. One such poetess is Pratibha Panghal. The pain of humans and birds is hidden in her poetry. The feeling of her poetry goes straight to the heart. Her lines work as a mirror to the society. She gives a big message to the people in very few words. Her first collection of poetry is being published. I pray that her poetry collection reaches the people and the feeling of her heart is on everyone's tongue.

Usman Minai Barabanki

Urdu Poet from Lucknow

Well written from the depths of pain and insight. She seems to have a fire of her own. It burns deep inside her one can tell from her words. I wish that she keeps on Writing.

_Steve Stone

Published poet, song writer and author from Ohio, United States. Most popular book SPLITTING DIOCHOTOMIES : My Therapy.

My ex-colleague and friend Pratibha has crafted a vibrant collection of relatable poems that touch upon various aspects of life. This book is a must-read and makes an excellent gift for friends.

This is just the beginning! Wishing her all the best and much success in life!

_Seema Dhawan

Managing Editor

Retropop Lifestyle Luxury Magazine

Listen to the Thorn Birds is an evocative collection of poems by my beloved, inspiring school teacher Pratibha madam. It almost feels like a painting of melancholy in subtle and muted colours. There is a lot to soak in, in between the lines

The less is more. Poetry lovers should give it a try.

Kanika Dhillon

Author,

Screenwriter

Producer

Founder @kathhapictures

www.ingramcontent.com/pod-product-compliance
Lightning Source LLC
LaVergne TN
LVHW061630070526
838199LV00071B/6639